THE SHIP AND THE STORM

THE SHIP
AND THE STORM

—

Poems by
Diane Callahan and David Dixon

Story Garden Publishing

This publication was made possible by generous funds from the Artist Projects Grant through the Greater Columbus Arts Council. Our heartfelt thanks to GCAC, the Columbus Mayor, Columbus City Council members, and Franklin County Commissioners for their support of the arts in Columbus.

**GREATER COLUMBUS
ARTS COUNCIL**

ISBN: 978-1-957627-50-2 (ebook)
ISBN: 978-1-957627-51-9 (paperback)
ISBN: 978-1-957627-52-6 (hardback)

CONTENTS

Diane ⬱

Dave ✦

II. Storm

III. Discovery

IV. Return

PREFACE

Writing this preface, in many ways, resembled writing the collection itself—lots of discussions, messages, and debates about intent, form, and meaning. One of us (we won't say which) initially doubted there should be a preface at all, but the other countered that as unknown writers, we need *some* sort of introduction, if only to justify why we structured the collection as we did, to explain that our poems are not randomly arranged across the page from one another but exist in *conversation* with each other. We went back and forth as we do in our poems, taking turns sometimes being the ship tossed about on the other's preferences, and at other times being the storm, attempting to convince our co-author by emotional appeal, protest, and occasionally just volume.

But in the end, the preface came together like our poems do. That is to say, with a little of each of us. The pieces in *The Ship and the Storm* are not always linked by theme or structure, and rarely is one poem a direct answer to another, but they reveal our hopes, fears, and worldviews. The pairings highlight our similarities and differences—and paradoxically, it is those differences that make our work truly shine together.

Diane is a poet who values beauty in language, in metaphor and imagery, while Dave is a "more obvious" poet, as he puts it. This dynamic was perhaps best illustrated during an editing session where Dave called out what he felt was a beautiful but overly complicated and unclear metaphor in Diane's work. She defended it on its aesthetic merits, and, mildly exasperated, he asked, "What is your obsession with form?" She laughed and shot back, "What is *your* obsession with meaning?"

Ironically, when we asked ourselves what we hoped readers would take away from this collection, it was Diane who had meaning, who knew what she wanted, and Dave who found himself struggling to answer. Diane said she hoped her poems would inspire the same sort of love and joy for poetry and the written word as other poets inspired in her, while Dave said he didn't really know and that, sometimes, he felt it might be easier for readers to explain to *him* what he was trying to do rather than the other way around.

Poets and writers of all stripes can be self-indulgent (after all, of the many words spoken and written every day, it takes a special sort of person to feel that theirs are worth showing to others), and we recognize that human folly. But whether it's beauty, meaning, or a little of both, we hope you find something here that speaks to you.

Ultimately, we understand that of all the written forms, poetry is perhaps the most dependent on you, the reader, as you will bring your own history and experiences to what you read, with our poems providing a lens through which to see the world. What it is you choose to look at is up to you.

—Diane and Dave

I
NAVIGATION

the patterns, the contradictions

after Lucille Clifton

i am swimming into myself
over and over again
lover to the riverbed
cold, so cold, but smooth
i am walking alone at night
walking into the near future
where no one holds my hand
with fear of losing me
i am talking to ghosts
made lighter in light
of secrets lost
a translucid ghost-talker;
goodbye thinning hair,
shoelaces i keep tripping over
i am leaving breadcrumbs
of hurt behind me
leaving the staying place
to carve desire paths
through my life.

Go Toward What Makes You Feel Most Alive

is what I got when
I asked an author to give
me some life advice

and it's good advice—
don't get
me wrong—but
I think it's the sort of
clever advice that
means different things to
different people

because as for me, I was once
in a country so far
across the expanse of geography and history that
it was on another planet

and on that other planet under
a moon most malevolent
and unfamiliar I
stumbled into a ditch of
waist-high weeds
backlit by
the pyre I had only
just escaped from

my face and their faces
cast in white and orange
by muzzle flashes—ours
and theirs—the
zip zip zip of death nipping
at our ears as it passed
and the snap and snarl of the
death we sent back to them

and in that ditch of weeds
I felt alive

most alive.

Inniswood

i.

Crouched by the frog pond,
I counted the tadpoles until I ran out
of numbers. Even then
I understood
only a few would become
the croaks we'd catch by the boardwalk,
slimy skin barely glimpsed
in murky mud.

At the stone bridge where the river
runs, you'd tell me to pick
my stick and
we'd race to the other side
like the storybook and you'd sigh,
Here today, gone tomorrow,
in your best mournful impression.

The moon was full on our walk when
you told me you never wanted children
but that the three of us were
the best choice you'd ever made.

I see us in the flowers—dahlias, mostly,
and tea roses, the deepest shades,
brides trying not to dust their trains.

ii.

Purple puff balls on stalks of green
straight out of Dr. Seuss—
alliums, I learn, belong to the onion family,
and the bird with the mottled belly,
voice like a clear stream:
the wood thrush. Someday
I would miss the
smell of lemon mint but not know
where to find it.

When I was thirteen, I asked you
while we played backyard badminton,
What happens when we die?
You were quiet for a moment,
then you said you weren't ever sure
but that we went back to the earth.

One night, the Sky Woman sculpture
was stolen from the turtle's back
and I could've sworn they found her
in two drunkards' dumpster.

iii.

I have been here every year of my life.
I've run these paths in the rain,
cursed mosquito bites in these forests,
been held bridal style in those tulip beds,
made scavenger hunts of counting stones,
worn the misty shroud of the secret garden.

But now is the time for marigolds
and I want to ask you if you've
ever gazed upon a gazebo like this one
made of wooden slats and a round
window you could almost
step through
and portal your way out.

iv.

You tell me about the barred owl
perched in broad daylight. I thought
I might've seen it years ago.
The hellebores are here and
my sister says we should get
matching tattoos that say
quiet
because of that oftentimes-answer
to how your day went:
Oh, I don't know—kind of quiet.

Your granddaughter runs ahead of us,
following the flow of invisible waterfalls.
I want to teach her words like *trellis*
and *lattice.*
I want to see it all again.

The Rapture

In my younger years, I used to live
in fear of the rapture coming

any day now. Back then I went to sleep
each night afraid that when I woke

my parents would be gone, taken
to heaven while I was left here on Earth,

given in to the hands of the Enemy,
lost forever. It all seems silly,

that pointless terror and constant dread
of promised judgment, since

I know now there's no end
to anything. It just keeps on going

and going and going. Jesus is not
coming to judge the world, will not

spare the righteous while punishing
the deserving wicked. No, if there is

any sparing or punishing
to be done, we, the righteous and wicked both,

must do it ourselves.
The end that saves us will never arrive.

How to Know Someone

First you ask them, *What is it about you that reminds me of something?* Never define what that something is. If it is undefinable, you can't be wrong. Try to pinpoint what it is anyway and give it a simple label like *tenderness* or *sea glass* or *Madonna* (the iconography or the icon). Remember that this person is human. Fallible. Without meaning to, you've boxed them inside a glass display case with a warm spotlight, which is flattering on the complexion but very claustrophobic. Put them somewhere else in the house, such as on the corner table you haven't known what to do with for years, then, like that corner table, bring them into conscious awareness only on rare occasions and wonder, *Does that belong somewhere else?* Don't fall for this. You must admit in therapy that anything that seemed remotely true about them was as far off the mark as when you thought penguins and polar bears existed on the same continent. Your coordinates were drawn on a map that will no longer guide you anywhere. Ask your mother; she knows. When you wander toward your own reflection, Narcissus, drink it up. You won't die if you stare too long. You'll only be forgotten, and forgetfulness is knowledge that was once held.

The Penguin Dictionary of Symbols

has been sitting on my shelf for years,
thick like a phonebook, promising
to decode so much of life—
the colors in the sky,
the fox on the sidewalk,
the number of miles between
me and where my children live—
and yet its spine remains uncracked.

I don't know if my life could stand
the cold gaze of a semiotician, one who views
the world as reference, sign
and portent;

most days I don't
know if it means
anything, and on the days I think
it does, I'd rather

not know.

what didn't burn in the sun

while the other kids held / the magnifying
glass above / the parading ants / I sprinkled
trails of cracker crumbs / watched them
carry the cargo across / sidewalk lines
transfixed by the traffic / of a thousand
little lives right outside / my parents' garage
where my dad wondered / why the troops
kept coming back

East of al-Muthana

       I was born
in a thunderclap
       a flash of fire and smoke and steel
that shook the earth
       like gods awakening.

       East of the mighty Tigris
I was killed
       in a blast like the final trumpet
sounding our doom
       like the end of the world.

In that moment
       of cordite and blood
shrapnel and flame

I was living
and dead
all at once.

I am still

east of the al-Muthana Bridge
east of the mighty Tigris.

Watch Me

      i.   up, up, down, down

My brother gave me his controller,
     taught me
     how to be a purple dragon
     and rescue my kin. When
my dragonfly companion began to hurt,
     he'd take over, save me
     from my fear of dying, of never making it
     past the first world. He wanted
someone to watch him save the kingdom.
We had no mind for clocks. I'd savor Capri-Sun
and squished spheres of white bread, pupils
shrunken before the screen's radiance. One time I

      ii.   left, right, left, right

sulked to my room because
we were supposed to take turns, but he
knocked on my door,
     brought me back.
When he was baptized in his roommate's
tub, I thought I'd lost him to God and
debates about how lines could be drawn. He forgave me
the time I overwrote
     his memory card
     for a game I began

and of course never finished. We danced
until the lamps shook, until pink and blue
arrows crawled behind our eyelids. My brother
is a reverse Pinocchio of sorts: he tells the truth

       iii.   B, A, Start

and my problems grow. Like the time I asked
      him not to tell how I cracked
the garage door with my Ford Taurus, but our parents
asked what happened.
      Only honesty lives in his mouth. Don't tell,
but he once wrote that he wanted
      to discover a new species of bird.
We'd milk rosebud and spend our spoils
on pools without guardrails, chemistry sets
      that turned us into monsters. Now
it's midnight again and we're
collecting the last gems. He glances
over his shoulder to make sure
I'm still watching.

The Eminent 310

Every time I hear the first notes of
"Shine On You Crazy Diamond,"
when that electric synth organ

emerges

out of nothing and swells like the thoughts of God
into a sound cold and lonely and yet
so close it's inside me and
every cell vibrates to its tune,
it takes me back to another time and place
more reliably than any tea-dipped madeleine
ever could.

Back to 1987, back to the great
monstrosity of my dad's synth organ:
an Eminent 310 in the corner of the living room.

Back to playing with its switches and knobs and
keys, trying to coax from it
something like music.

He doesn't play anymore—
didn't much then—and I don't even remember
what happened to the organ.

I'm sure I could ask my dad where it went,
but the answer is moot
because, like childhood, once a thing like
that is gone
it is gone.

Sisters

I wander into your bedroom,
every artifact in motion:
mud dries on dark cleats,
milk curdles in a cereal bowl,
and inside a case flung open
a trumpet worships Miles Davis.

From under your mattress, I steal
a love letter written on notebook
paper and your favorite pair
of polka dots.

Standing on my maroon bedspread,
velvet like royalty, I unfurl
a treasure map of the world
bordered with Italian fountains,
Greek domes. I cover every blank wall
with tiny extensions of how I am
different from you:

a keychain shaped like a pierced tongue,
baby Lucifer in red yarn, a poster
of the metal-armed alchemist I kiss
every night beneath glowing
ceiling stars.

Sister, I will tell the truth:
there has never been a time
when I didn't feel far from you
yet here you are
holding your stomach
with laughter before I've even
finished the joke.

Jazz Impressions

In 1989
I am a young man.

A boy, really,

riding with my grandfather
in his big gray Lincoln
that floats like a boat on the sea.

We drive east in the empty dark
toward Wilmington,
toward the coast.

And in the night as we speed along—
jazz.

The voice on the radio is
tobacco cured
and honey sweet:
"And now, my fellow travelers in the dark,
some Miles Davis for you."

And we listen,
young boy growing older
and old man
returning to his youth,
to Miles Davis and Ornette Coleman
and John Coltrane.

All My Knowledge of the Bible

comes secondhand, from Buckley singing
she broke his throne & cut his hair
but Cohen sang it first. All my songs were born
wearing another voice. I'm made of
impressions I don't recognize. I learned of Cain's curse
from Steinbeck—nobody told me
what I'd find east of Eden & I never really hungered
to know because my least favorite rooms in museums
bleed iconography & I sneeze at gold leaf—give me
a Rothko over a Rubens any day. It's not disdain
but a lack of reverberation, like seeing the sign for Jerusalem
on a country highway, or drinking a glass
of lukewarm water
when you're not thirsty.

Proust

What to say about an author who has insights on love,
jealousy, longing, and desire so profound and so universal
while at the same time so personal as to have lived the
reader's own life but who also cannot resist explaining
everything, from a coachman waiting at a door to a
dizzyingly innumerable array of party guests who will not
be seen for the remainder of the novel or even the rest of
the scene with page after page of description which is itself
merely described in terms of something else, be it Greek
myth or a painting, sculpture, or sonata contemporary to
Proust's time which will have you, dear reader, scurrying
back across both footnotes and nine or ten dependent clauses,
across sentences that never seem to end, sentences doubling
back on themselves like S-curves in a river or perhaps an
Oxbow lake, almost but never quite touching so that you've
nearly lost where his original thought began, and so his
insight and genius and depth of feeling, which is no doubt
astonishing, is lost underneath a veritable avalanche of words
and descriptions and discursive thoughts, as if you are trying
to gather your thoughts while staring at velvet-patterned
wallpaper behind a vase of lilacs sitting upon a mantle in
a room full of dim candles which call to mind late nights
waiting on your mother to say goodnight, and surrounded
by bric-a-brac in the old Empire style of Napoleon III as
was popular in some never-time before you were born, all of
which is only half-lit in the gloom of your mistress's burning
oil lamp which is now almost out because you are waiting
for her to return to her bed from where she is outside in the

hall talking in a low voice to someone who has knocked
on her door at night but whom her servants say is no one,
although you cannot trust them because, after all, they are in
her employ as surely as are all the gods in the employ of the
Fates themselves, cutting the strings like so many strands
of wayward hair, like the very gray ones your mistress must
have cut from her head between when you saw her last night
at Mme. Verdurin's and today, even though she claims she has
done nothing but be in bed sick the whole time?

Barbara,

meaning stranger; meaning plastic doll; meaning
Aqua on repeat teaching me hanky-panky.

Meaning the name that was given to me, gifted, meaning
a grandmother's—my grandmother's
        (no, I can't sing, not yet);
meaning *it's spelled bar-bar-a* and a mental box
of chocolate bars, a whole stack of them,
and if you sell enough you'll earn a big prize like
a one-size-fits-all baseball cap or a half-hearted
VHS player; not *bra*, too big
for my breasts, like dinner plates for a single
sunny-side up;

meaning barbarian, meaning savage, really
meaning foreign, with barbarous customs,
eating mashed potatoes and gravy with
my naked fingers until I was twelve;

meaning Rhabarberbar, buying whatever's needed to make

strawberry rhubarb pie for my mama, tart
and sweet like summer—
the cashier asked what it was, said,
It looks like pink celery!

Meaning the opposite of or perhaps synonymous with divine
    (no, I won't let down my curls, not ever);

meaning
a tower-bound saint, why I've never been struck
by lightning.

On an Epigraph

The door was open but the way was not lit.
—**Lee Ranaldo**

I read you a poem—
not this one—
and your response was

silence. Finally,
after an awkward
moment, you told me
in the sweetest voice

I like the epigraph.

So that is what
remains.

August

That hedge out front
saved my mother's life
when she, eight months
round with me,
fell sideways off the stoop she
couldn't see, but
Mother Earth caught her,
        caught me.

With years, that hedge overtakes
our walkway, makes it impossible
to ignore, untamable like
        the life it saved
(like daughter, like mother)
yet we prune it dead
shear off the arms
where once we could fall
        so gently.

Christmas 1989

Years and years ago,
at least one decade if
not more,
well before James and Kenzie were alive
and back when Nina still was,
you pulled out a
family Christmas album
from the late 80s for us
to look at—four by sixes
of me with some space Legos
and little green army men,
Jonathan in a red cowboy hat
with a six-shooter cap gun,
and Katie just a baby
all in pink;
the house wasn't even finished,
not like it is now. No,
in the pictures it will always be
the construction zone
it was for my entire childhood.
And as we looked it over
you asked

with tears in your eyes

you had a good childhood,
didn't you?

We said *yes, of course*.

Later Jonathan and I
shook our heads at how
sentimental you were
as we wondered what
had brought that on.

And I just want you to
know, should you
still nurse that question
deep down in your soul, that
while I have never said
I love you
when I didn't mean it,

there have been plenty of times
when I meant it
but didn't say it.

II
STORM

Some Changes May Not Be Saved

1.

Through your eyes, let me
see everything you see now:
dreams of the Korengal
the moral calculus of rounds from a rooftop
a warm loaf of beer bread formed
by your tired hands
a woman who condemns men
to that pleasant fog of memory
recalled with a kind but distant smile.

2.

I told your son last night
how it wasn't that you were frustrated
with him
it's just that fathers worry
about not being good enough
teachers. If a child steps
into the waiting maw of the world
and it devours the meat from his bones
leaves him cold and skinless
the father will be to blame
for not bestowing the right sword
because no one can hide from the world
nor tame it.

3.

Do you believe writing should be
a solitary endeavor?
All these retreats and residencies
seem to think we must
ruminate in our rustic cabins
carry pails of feed for the pigs
boots wet with farm mud
as we walk the path alone
sleep on a hard bed
alone. I once heard an author advise
sex will only distract you;
marry someone who wants it
once a week, at most. I can only bear to look at us
sideways. Take a picture for me.
Send it years from now. Tell me what it's like
to hide yourself as an artist, a being
for whom hiding one's true self
is exquisitely painful.

4.

I wrote my last wishes—I want to be good
for the environment.
A tree for a headstone. All those books
must go somewhere.
The library we've built
together will birth a scattering
of smaller libraries. You will no longer be able
to look at my shelves
and know me.
People will need to be informed, although
the guest list is a revolving door.
But what to do
about things left unfinished: the conversations,
the stories.

Last Night, I Dreamed of the Korengal

boulders like giants' teeth
the kind that will grind your bones for bread
jut from the ridge like
molars from a bleached jawbone
in profile against
green terraces draped over the hillsides
like a silk robe on the floor
while above me the tall necks of pines
tower to the sky
dappling the forest with the light of an afternoon
perhaps the last afternoon

the dark windows of flat-roofed houses
skulls with empty eye sockets
stare down at us
the stare of the dead
at those who soon will join them

bullets snap around me like the angriest of hornets
stingers of copper, venom of lead

overhead the four-bladed locusts hover
stings in their tails
as prophesied by John of Patmos
but even he
in his wildest fever dreams of sickness or madness
could not have

dreamed of the Korengal

Care Instructions

Go to the beach—Hilton Head
probably, that surf shop where, next to the *Beach
Bum* T-shirts, sit too-small glass
tanks of neon shells, dry sponges, and
hermit crabs with matchstick legs. Cradle
one in your too-small palm. Back home
build him a Lego mansion
four stories tall but with steps for
climbing and windows for the cat to watch
and pellet trails leading to the labyrinth's
exit. Frown at the highlighter-yellow
shell, how dirty it gets in the sand,
and take your pet
to the bathroom sink, the one with the
faucets that are hard to turn. Give
the hermit crab a bath in hot water
that feels good against your skin but
watch all his little legs fall
down the drain and hold
the empty shell between your fingers
hold it still.
Grow older and learn how they shed
their exoskeletons and how fragile
they are at this time and how their life-
span is decades, not six months, how
the sand must be deep, and how much
they need other hermits.

9 Line

DUSTOFF, this is SABER THREE SIX. Prepare to copy Nine Line Medevac request. OVER.

SABER THREE SIX, DUSTOFF, ROGER. Prepared to copy. OVER.

LINE ONE: (Location) One Eight Sierra Uniform Juliet Two Two Two Six Zero Four Six Niner Six BREAK

LINE TWO: (Callsign/Frequency) SABER THREE SIX; Single Channel Plain Text Two Five Four Three One Niner Four Two One Zero BREAK

LINE THREE: (# Patients by Precedence) One; Urgent— urgent usually meaning the patient will expire within two hours if not treated, but this is a chronic sort of urgency, an urgency that lasts from the moment you realize it's there until it kills you BREAK

LINE FOUR: (Special Equipment Required) Uniform November Kilo—god I wish I knew; I wish there was some sort of special equipment; god knows I've tried everything— the bottle and the tennis shoes and the typewriter and the television and the couch BREAK

LINE FIVE: (# Patients by Type) One; Alpha—that is, ambulatory, at least most days anyway, although there've been some times, if I'm being honest, that I just don't BREAK

LINE SIX: (Security of PZ) Echo—enemy in area; proceed with caution, which is definitely true because this patient is a danger to himself, he's his own adversary, and he's looking at himself down the sights BREAK

LINE SEVEN: (Method of Marking PZ) The Black Humor of a Depressed Person—you can mark a PZ with anything, but if nobody else has their eyes open it doesn't really matter what you mark it with BREAK

LINE EIGHT: (Patient Nationality and Status) Alpha—US Military, or was, anyway, once upon a time, and still is, in his mind, at least BREAK

LINE NINE: (Contamination) November; Bravo; Charlie—nuclear, biological, and chemical, which seems like a lot but it's all there, if you think about it; don't bother wearing your suit though, it's every fucking where these days anyway OVER

SABER THREE SIX, this is DUSTOFF. Say again?

Makeup Palette

Dipping into those shades of my body
the labia pinks, polished collarbone, freshly
bruised knees, left armpit mole
the lights and darks, colors I can't blend
or won't
trying them on for someone else
when I'd rather be colorless

like air, breathable,
and on my own
I'll mix as I please.

Reading Bukowski on the Bus

you shouldn't read Bukowski on the bus
because all you want to do when you read
Bukowski is fight or fuck.

but you're just on the way to earn
your check like you did yesterday
and no matter how much you want to fight
or fuck
you're not going to do either one

and that will gnaw at your guts the rest of the day like
a hungry rat going through a bag in the trash
to get at what's left
of a half-eaten burger.

Heartsore

you were moving like pond water this morning
all surface tension and stillness
a depression in the ground filled
with standing water
but you do not want to stand anymore

what you want is to split the trees
with your destructive whims
so restless in the ancient grove
so restless all your life

every morning is the pond
it is scrubbing dirt from fingernails
pulling hairs from the bristles of a brush
letting skin become dust
then you leave
fingernails and brushes and self
at the bottom of that waiting water

Struggle

The mist rises from the pavement

like steam from a prizefighter
who's gone nine rounds
with his rival

thrown his punches
with all he has
nothing left inside
left it all on the canvas

his blood and water mingling
together like
the holiest of offerings
an atonement for his sins.

And like the prizefighter
the battered earth sits
exhausted
spent
waiting for a decision
waiting to see if the struggle

ends in victory
or defeat.

Separation

when the thought arrives / as timely as a train in Tokyo /
I feed it / twelve strokes of luck / miniature erasers in the
shape of foods you liked / chocolate-covered doughnuts and
strawberry shortcake / chainsaws / a white cat who doesn't
answer / to any of the names you call her / a sick beat / that
sickens me now / I have a particular daydream / not of hot
baths / my maligned travel guides / holding your hand up
the temple steps / but of the plane ride home / of you snoring
into the aisle / and I don't even / poke you awake / just let you
make noise / be as loud as your shirts / be mine

The Light and the Flower

while we talk about why things are ending I
stare
at the light on the ceiling and
open
my eyes wide
to its overwhelming brightness
that lets nothing hide

when I close them
what remains
is the glowing vision of an orchid
clothed in unnatural violet
against the night-black nothing

a memory in the dark
of what is not

The Way You Talk About War

your eyes, they
sing like a soldier marching south
but your fists betray how it pains you to be
fluent in the language of violence, how
it hurts to dust blood-stained soil
from your boots

because you know
when a quiet man dies
one day in December
on the wings of a black bird
the world hears nothing
but heat, gunfire, and loss,
that none of it
means
a goddamn thing

War Poetry

rifles fire
in staccato rhythm:

bullets snapping in lines
that sing

and sting.

machine guns argue back and forth
like lovers.

desperate orders are
earnest haikus
the quiet in the loud.

reloads our enjambments.

On a Whim

Delete every version of yourself all the pixels of thought X's mar
the spots you no longer want to be touched arms cradle air nothing
can escape the skin, not even a name, and one sunny afternoon
while weeding the garden you will forget whose hand holds
the trowel an improbable schism of body and mind but one can
destroy the self on a whim.

Constituent Parts

the barrel's just a tube of steel and block
while the frame is incomplete like scaffolding
and the magazine is useless
the slide the top half of an old animal skull
not even complete enough to frighten
and the rest all springs and rods
that could have come from a toy

but

as you make the whole
out of all those innocuous pieces
the demon slowly assembles

ready

wherever it is pointed

be it at a friend by accident
or a brother or a wife by design

or to a temple for the very last time

to disassemble
their constituent parts

When the Power Goes Out

everybody's asking what I need

and Joy is singing about keeping the light on
and I'm at the concert alone as the temperature drops below
the number of days it's been since I went to bed
before two in the morning

I left the cats behind with their built-in blankets
and all the groceries I finally bought after a month of
getting by on stale sandwiches and frost-burned perogies
and my car engine dies in the front parking lot

the Uber driver is telling me about the guy high
on dentistry saying he's horny, about
the humanities professor
crying in his backseat because her visa was revoked,
and Joy is wiping her tears on stage
because the *Tribune* wrote
her unpolished performance was
too sincere and kind
to be believed

and when Joy says, *Sometimes I don't feel like I'm enough,*
the crowd shouts back, *You are! You are enough!*
and when I come home, it is all light and heat but

none of that is what I needed, because as I told you
later that night, when I had collected all the
electric candles and put away my winter coat,
I only need people to ask me the question
while Joy sings me to sleep.

The Office Christmas Party

Dear Diane I think
I already told you but
maybe I forgot or perhaps you
did so here it is again: yesterday
was our office
Christmas party which is
a surreal moment anywhere I guess.

My normally buttoned-up
coworkers in ugly sweaters and Santa
hats or a lime green velvet Grinch suit
drinking eggnog from the punch bowl
or beers from a cooler in the hall
in the middle of the workday.

But it's especially odd given
my profession;
it forms
a strange sort of incongruence to be
one moment watching foreign
news with an anxious eye
on bombed-out
rubble in Aleppo or Rafah or
Donetsk,
and that as a break from cataloguing
numbers of missiles fired and troops deployed

and the next moment celebrating
the birth of the Prince of Peace

in a crowded Pentagon hallway.

Brood Parasite

The cowbird cares only for her own
propagation. Nest-stealer, child-trader.
A clutch of brown-spotted eggs
sheltered elsewhere. The cowbird
merely uses what others have created.
Others raise her children.
Others feed her young.
If her child stabs a fragile fledgling
from the colonized species
with a beak that hungers for more,
this is no injustice.

The brood parasite
has no reason to question
her good fortune
in finding the nest she
occupies, takes from,
ruins.

Most hosts know this song:
All I want is to live here
and not think of other eggs,
other birds. Why must I
think of them?

After all, the cowbird is native
to the Great Plains, as American as bison.
When she eats before the rest,
the cowbird
does not see herself as a parasite.

Horses Will Eat Themselves to Death

long after a horse is full
it will keep eating
as long as there's more
to consume

it will eat until the grain ferments
in its stomach—
too much
too rich—
or until its hooves
collapse and
it can't stand up

greed will kill a thing

Roadkill

What scared me most
about the stranger—the glint-eyed boy

who grabbed my arm on the far-from-home
thoroughfare of Grafton Street, who

spoke words to me I froze to hear
before my classmate pulled me away

calmer than needed, and the stranger
dissolved down the stream of people—

was what it taught me about myself:
that I was no stronger than a deer

carcass on the roadway, the same
kill for which I'd place a hand over my heart

in benediction every time I drove past,
pitying the dead for the encroachment

of man. Yet I was an animal too,
I was prey too, I could be

predator if I remembered my teeth, but all I had
were beady eyes and a cottonwood tail and

thin legs that would not move even if
everything in me screamed.

Look at This Thing We've Made

I.

Wife
Look at this thing
we've made
toothless, shriveled, red-faced, howling
at the world
with every breath
we love it as we've never loved
anything else
this perfect child we've only just met
yet now could never bear to part from

II.

Daddy
Look at this thing
I've made
a picture of a brown horse galloping
across a narrow strip of green grass
white house on the left
with four pink windows
the sky coming down blue like the sea
to meet the grass and the horse
and the house
blue filling up every crevice
blue like her eyes wide when she smiles
isn't it beautiful

of course it is
it's the most beautiful thing I've ever seen
and it hangs now on the refrigerator
next to last week's spelling test
and drawing of a unicorn in the snow

III.

My son
Look at this thing
I've made
long and cold
all black steel, aluminum
grooved and machined
to perfect precision, tolerances
a tenth of a millimeter
slide the magazine into the well
pull back the charging handle
let it go
hear how it slides
hear that satisfying snap
the round riding home into the chamber
see this here
wherever that red dot is
that's where the bullet goes
easy
with this in your hands you need never fear
nor worry

you are a man among your fellow men
son of Ares himself

IV.

Class
Look at this thing
you've made
poster for the classroom door
so everyone knows it's us
Mrs. Foster's Wiggleworms
a picture you've each drawn of yourselves
hair standing on tops of heads and
glasses too big for faces
smiles nothing more than little curved lines
dots for eyes
and each of you did so well
adding a picture of something you love
yellow and brown triangles with red circles
Pokémon and Captain America's shield
golden sun above pink flowers
a drawing of the beach
blue waves meeting
a line of brown sand
I love it
Wiggleworms

V.

America
Look at this thing
we've made
holes in the wall
pockmarks in the cinderblock
splinters of the door blasted into the hallway
broken glass from windows
designed in other times by unwitting architects
to let in sunlight
so children would feel connected
to the wider world around them
but which instead admitted
the gaze of inchoate rage
floor slick with blood
in lines where bodies earlier so bright with promise
were dragged
by their classmates
teachers
police
strangers to another room
to be identified

Look at this thing
we've made

III
DISCOVERY

Find Me a Savior

Women like you get hurt because
the crucifix allows men
to forget, because
it isn't your fault, but you hate
yourself anyway as you sit alone
on stone steps waiting for
a verdict that won't stitch
          the tear, and you
imprint your grandmother's
cross in ink where lace
defends it, delicious blasphemy
akin to a confessional and
you delight in the female form,
your form,
because the hypnosis of your hips
belongs to you, no matter what others
have claimed, because looking in the
mirror is a lot like loving a self
you have yet to meet.

In Your Shade

I spent years in your shadow
underneath what you claimed was
the protective umbrella of God's good grace,
Him above you and you
above us, sheltering
us from—what, exactly, I don't remember. Because
a little rain

never hurt anyone.

Tell me,
when you touched her
and her and her and who knows
how many other hers
did you tell yourself you were
sheltering them from something worse? Or did
you know

that what you sheltered us from was
not the storm but the light
—light that would have
revealed to us those
things which you did not want us to see.

We grew sickly in your shade, impotent, but
when she screamed, we were forced

to stumble out into the bright world of the living.

Bodies

after you cut
down the dead
    trees
the field yawns
and gives for the first
time in twenty years
    a glimpse
of red beyond the shuddering
loblollies—decaying
metal and wood teeth,
the remains of man's work.

beside a stump:
    a gray body
shell of skin
we count the bands
six, no, seven
marvel at the armor
    left behind.

we trudge homeward
talking of terrace
    gardens
what we could do with
all this nakedness, till you meet
    the skeleton
of that copse of pines
which once harbored your

cage-eyed
calico who, startled by noise,
jumped from the deck and
        cowered there.

that night
flashlight in hand
you found her in the needles
        and brought her inside.

After "Rusty Cage"

I ran away
looked over my shoulder
at the strip of road cut
through the spruces
for a moment my eyes
shining gold in god's headlights
for

I broke my rusty cage

to flee the false light of
being known

for the real
darkness of knowing

myself and others we
found in the night

small dark truths in their closeness

hiding galaxies brighter than a million
morning suns

Metamorphic

paintings that try to be what they aren't—
      skulls of bread, calla lilies masquerading as feminine
faces, me pretending to be the sky

everything strives to become something else
      like the acoustic mimicry of moths, their ultrasonic
mutterings like false flags, a promised bitterness

I am the girl with moths for eyes
      fingers stained with life, a smile so serene it's sinful,
gazing up at whatever is brighter

lie to me, fool me, please
      some of us do not have mouths just caves aching to be
vessels or megaphones

Apophenia

of course I love you
why would you think any different

a sharp-winged gull
dives from its place against the deep blue sky
and plunges into the sea

Artless Man

Let's repeat an exercise from childhood.

Lie on this blanket of paper,
arms and legs splayed as you stare
at the speckled stars on the ceiling,
the caress of my pencil against your skin
bringing me close
enough to read the words
engraved on the silver band
hugging your wrist.

This is childhood in essence
where exploration means
seeking hands, widening
eyes, stretching limbs.

You call yourself an artless man
too far gone to learn the motions
of brushing color and stringing
words like beads, doomed to be
a lifeless tracing,
a body outlined in chalk.

                              Breathe slow.
                              Remember that no contours
                              define our shape,
                              save the ones
                              we draw ourselves.

jazz

not smooth jazz
not the kind they play in elevators
grocery stores
macy's
not that kind

not that kind
no

the kind that's all discordant horns
and pianos that thunder in
then fade out

only to return without warning

playing something different
than the rest of the band
drumsticks on cymbals
rain that won't stop
drowning out everything else
until a bass line thuds
and the horns blare
a quick shout of protest

or perhaps triumph
nobody really knows

that kind of jazz

the kind where you listen
for someone
to make something
out of all that
noise

You find an apology letter on your windshield

I'm sorry for how I doubted
you could learn, but
I was right after all—
you still don't want to be a mother;
you still chase novelty like a cat
chases anything with a will to live;
you keep having your lovers' quarrel with
the world, and you hold it and yourself
and every person accountable
to the high standards of fictional
universes where people change,
where growth means
immutable transformation.

Maybe you're just more you,
harder-tongued and softer-bellied,
more likely to succeed
at thirty-two than my seventeen.
More dreaming, more knowing,
more certain that
the next letter you write to yourself
will contain no trace of I-told-you-so,
but rather you will tell me
all the ways I read you wrong,
even though letters can't be
sent backward.

Sergio de la Pava Does Not Live in Brooklyn

At least that's what his
biography says on
the back of the book

I don't know where he lives
except it isn't Brooklyn

Like most other people
I also don't live in Brooklyn
which is fine with me

It isn't the center of
the universe even if everyone
I've ever met from Brooklyn
thinks it is

Flower Bud

are you afraid
of the little flower bud
that might
or might not
grow inside me?

or do you crave
the bloom
because it means
you and I
will, at long last,
nurture something together?

Blue Line

When I board the Blue Line
in Franconia the engineer
always promises this is the train

to Largo, a mystical place—

there the tracks end
and any traveler who dares press further
must do so on foot or horse or camel
perhaps

I imagine Largo as Shangri-la
or maybe even El Dorado
a lost city where the rooftops
gleam gold in the setting sun
her high priests finishing the ancient rites
just as the Metro car pulls in
brakes squealing like an animal
about to be sacrificed

Never have I been to Largo but
one day I will see it

for myself

The Mold

I've always wanted to be free in my life and art. It's as
important to me as truth.
—**Marisol Escobar**

she herself was her only mold
called vain for casting her face
in dead-eyed triggerfish and cocktail partygoers
i stare back
every woman seeing in herself other women, another woman
until the word unfolds itself into futility
until i am driving somewhere i don't need to go
foible-ridden like an old stoner
the last song of the night warns me
not to scroll too far back
not to reduce myself to the love of a man
to the hatred of men
to the violence of men

anxiety is the mark of history
of unlocked doors, of cocked guns
a little girl buried twice
my own shame a panopticon where I can't hide from
bodice rippers and honeyed teacups
i am at odds with my birth, fighting
softness, protected by fake laughter
at all his jokes, not going where my breed goes missing.

i dream of a woman with graying curls
i compliment her, say they look like mine
used to when i was young
she advises me to *be with the one*
who makes you feel young the longest. am i free?
can i trust that love isn't surrender?
why do i remember this way, give every slight the weight
of a dead sparrow in the snow?

woman
the word
feels leaden in my gut like too much sourdough
i want to cast my face onto the uncanny
where i can stare back at her
a woman seeing in herself another woman, other women.

I Told You to Ask Your Landlord

to fix your air conditioner
but you said no
refusing to
give in to a world that
had already taxed you too
much that week to
surrender again to
its demands
and when I asked if
refusal would fix
the air conditioner you
further refused to dignify
my impertinent question with an answer
and in the moment I thought
it was perhaps a bit silly but time
and you
have taught me that living is
defiance both
of what we can defeat
and of what we must
succumb to

that weekend was sweltering
but at least we sweltered
alive and with our eyes open
rather than giving in
to the cool and simple
end of things

Redwood

after Louise Glück

You are eyeing my skin;
is it because it is beautiful
and you envy me or
because it so resembles your own—
red and peeling and laid bare?
Or maybe you fail
to see me in my entirety,
so focused on your own hands
and what they are
doing with their time that you
don't even look up at my
branches, far above your
own, trying to show you
there is sky,
there is rain.

Answer Enough

after Stephen Crane

In the backyard,
A vulture as if on a gallows perched
Atop the fence,
And as he eyed me,
I asked him,
"Nothing is
Dead or nearly so. Why
Are you here?"

The cold gaze of his
Lidless black eye
Was answer enough.

Things I Never Want to Understand

a dog's tongue smitten with his human's face, the tapping hand
on a steering wheel, desert humor of saguaros waving too many
arms,

the sun cracking against the surface of stones shaped
like teapots and clothing irons, newlyweds braving the cliff's edge

to make promises and the pink petals they shed that feel smooth
as baby skin, finding a handwoven purse in the pews and pacing

the churchyard for a stranger who looks lost, maybe those grains
of sand beneath my fingernails, what I couldn't quite bring myself to
leave.

The Projects of Distracted Gods

The city at night is
lit from inside like a child's shoebox diorama
made for a school project
little windows cut out of cardboard.

And each of us?

A tiny cardstock figure
against the backdrop of
the city
on an errand—
coming home from work
or on our way out to the club—
determined to matter
to draw some fleeting attention
from a distracted god
done with his project
now only concerned with cleaning up the mess
so he can move on to something else.

Now shoving the whole city into the back of the closet
into the dark.

IV
RETURN

Senescence

i

Let me die like a sunflower
        on the roadside let it be a long
death let me die knowing
        I once turned toward the sun

My grandmothers survived
        on spoonfuls of peanut butter and pieces of iris
meaning the place you were planted is meaningless
        what you feed on most is alive in your guts

if you run your hand roughly over the surface
        pieces of us fall away

pieces of us

ii

Someday a girl
will glimpse me
                from a car window

                        and bow her head.

Magnolia Blooms

a starburst
amongst the many-possibilitied universes
folded and overlapping
so deep a green they are almost black
a flash of white and yellow
the blooms of the Big Bang
and the smell of creation

A Study in Lavender

Cut off your
      limbs, grow in new soil
we are the not-yet-
      bloomed, the shoot in your side
      they tell us to calm the nervous
system, so we make lavender lemonade
put a pot on to boil, one cup
      lemon juice, fresh lemons, two
cups water, cold water, strained
      sugar so you can swallow it down
      lavender on the wrists
of prostitutes, lavender on the tongues
of heretics, lavender days and nights
      at the cabaret we prune and prune
and prune, but it never softens the energy, only
      entices the open flame
      let us keep our domed shape and take
our sprigs to your neighbors, the one
with the weeded garden, the other
      who rules over mud, and to the stone
      houses still standing after
the wilting of time lavender will remain
      at the end of the world if you let
your fingers caress the dirt
      if you let its fragrance bleed
      into the harvest.
The seeds of flowers begin
      with your open palm.

Bradford Pear

a red pickup truck
too clean to have fulfilled the promise
of the commercials,
of climbing boulders to some distant
ridgeline to be crowned
triumphant, looking down across a nameless
barren valley somewhere in a West too featureless
and high definition not to be
enhanced by computers.
when you're selling trucks to suburban fathers
you have to remove all traces of
anyone else—
other people only remind you
that you aren't young anymore and you've
never been to the top of some faraway
mountain or even ascended the hill just
on the other side of the highway.
instead you live in the suburbs
surrounded by your fellow men, your truck
not gleaming under starlight's open
expanse but
instead reflecting the glow of
your neighbor's porch light
filtered
through the missing leaves
of his Bradford pear.

Perpetual Motion

time drifts, slips, shrinks,
fast and flighty as a hummingbird—
the wind transforms copper curls
into flames blazing wild. the sun
captures white fluffs of cottonwood drifting
in a summer snow so abundant
a seed might land on your tongue and grow
a tree inside you. a small, soft body
rises and falls as your name
makes new roads on my tongue.

Wrong End

when you're young, death
seems like such
a small figure
the Reaper so
far away
you need
a spyglass to see him.

it's only when you
get older
that you find you've
been looking through
the wrong end
of the telescope.

the pyre

for Nic

      if we didn't keep our homes in small ways
how they were Before
the half-burned candles and unworn futures inviting
alternate selves
      if we never wondered about our wandering souls
who drove through blizzards, trusting arrows to lead us
around Dead Man's Curve
      if we didn't walk on air every Christmas and
remember the heavy miracle of snow in Ohio
for a traveler who has only seen foam and paper
      if we never glimpsed peace in the distance
      never accepted that
      what once was will forever be

we would simply exist
as a pyre burning in memory
of the past.

The Pyre

you told me once
that all your other lovers
had let the flames of ardor
dwindle
down
to the weakest
of embers—
needed breath to even see them
glow against the ash.

determined not to lose the flame,
I threw my world upon the pyre.

now I fear in my desire
to never let the fire die
I've chopped and cut,
stripped you limb from limb,
and burned you up.

Micro Expressions

too busy living to hit record

I dread the day your
side-mouth impressions
        wry as a country song
slip from my ridges

and you
with freckles real or imagined
those teeth so honest
        eyes like a lightning strike
a fox's cackle, wicked

and you
the thinker in profile
long fingers on knowing hands
        the whir-click of hidden clockwork

I want to collect
every likeness in my pocket
an expression set in copper
like coinage

what if twenty years gone
        you are burnt up
        space rock stardust
not even named
not even a ghost?

Listening to Gershwin at the End of the World

In the light of tomorrow's
blood orange sun turning
the morning's icy purple clouds
into tiger-striped dawn
who knows what rough beast
is this future coming
to greet us?

But come it will, this cup
brimming with tomorrow's

tomorrow and all its children—
it cannot pass from us.

Eli, Eli, lama sabachthani,
though the choice was ours.

But for now, it is just
another cold night
of sitting on the couch
watching the snow fall
as the neighbors set out
their trash for the
morning's early pickup, just
another night of listening
to Gershwin and waiting
for the end
of the world.

Running Through the Memory Gardens

a path through the cornfield, and I follow it

footsteps sinking in soft soil, ears of dark gemstones
dry stalks reaching out to remember skin
a trail leading between the dead and living

empty tombs in the underbrush, fake flowers
casual as old tires and left-behind loveseats
trees caught in a state of flux, vivified
every oak sings through the lungs of windchimes

at the end
of the cemetery lane
framed in the mausoleum glass
the marble-white statue of an embrace—
time stretches to contain everything we are

while a woman visits a newly born graveside, I detour
through a field of golden chanterelle, an honor
to be a home for life someday
please don't read too much into the wilting dahlias
the blur of black feathers overhead

legs burning, I run counterclockwise
back to the other side
fresh mulch, rain-soaked sidewalk
a stagnant butterfly on concrete, blue-speckled wings
the milkweed pods at the house where a family

was murdered a memory ago
bursting with seeds

three boys guide skateboards up the hill
ride down the road's slant, no fear of finality
I wave to the old woman who sits on a folding chair
smoking in the shade of her garage

passing other aching, breathing people
makes me run farther, longer
I swing right, listen for the lilt of my lavender,
my morning glories crying for light,
a familiar voice vining the doorway, and far away

the chimes, the chimes, the chimes.

The Fox at the Corner of First Landing and Burke Center Parkway

Golden-eyed
    and cloaked in red
he watches from the sidewalk

as unsure
    of my hidden
intent as I am of his

so we stare
    at each other
until he loses interest

and slinks into
    the darkened wood,
his golden eyes the last I

see of him.
    I hope he sees me
smile as he goes; after

all, I took
    this lonely stroll
just to see his bushy tail.

patagium

the old morning was a house sparrow
building nests in the gutter. the new morning is not
a bird at all but a bat, unfolding at night, with small
eyes, sensing the way through echoes.

someone posed the question *what are you*
willing to commit to unmovingly?
the membrane of my wings is thin. you are
my reason for flying. you are

all I am willing.

In That Tiny Bar Off Dock Street

candlelight tints the carnations red
mirrored walls reflecting you
from a dozen
different angles
I watch you
pen to paper
craft a poem in the company
of your cocktail
at a table too small to
hold your thoughts that
flower like the carnations like
the flame like
the dancing shadows in my glass
of gin.

Radial

Here is every lie ever told

        I will always be there for you

     a glimpse of red beyond the shuddering loblollies

You'll never be alone   pieces of us fall away

a kind but distant smile   I want what's best for you

          You never do anything right

     It's all your fault   on the wings of a black bird

     pieces of us fall away   like a silk robe on the floor

the fox on the sidewalk   You didn't do anything wrong

        the end that saves us will never arrive

my fellow travelers in the dark   Everything happens for a reason

the heavy miracle of snow   She took the first bite

            only honesty lives in his mouth

He had no idea any of this was happening

You have no one to blame but yourself

so restless all
your
life

The First Clenched Fist

you have probably heard of Cain
who slew his brother Abel in some
distant field
across the empty and forgotten
centuries

the first to mark our kind
with the stain of blood
we have never been able
to wash out.

first murderer though he may be
he was not the first to clench his
fist.

because you see to grasp Eve's
hand Adam had to
let go of the Lord's.

then the great Creator of Heaven and Earth
scorned in favor of that
which He Himself created
clenched His fist
and banished us from
Paradise's Garden.

we have been wandering
from that day on
paradise all but forgotten.

but the fist?

that we remember.

it has been clenched
ever since.

And Sometimes It Feels Like We Never Left

When I come back to haunt
the house on Abbey Avenue
I can no longer smell just-born croissants,
can no longer feel the want
that kept me tied to the upper window
where storms brewed hot like coffee
you made just for your mother on
weekend visits that you always said
were too long, and the guest bed grew
fertile with sunflowers, and we grew into our
wrinkles but not each other. When I
come back to float under the archways
of the house on Abbey Avenue
this time I have no plans to leave.
The hopeful pumpkins pushing through the fence slats
need me, and so does the sun alighting through the glass
into my ghost library, and someone must
refill the birdseed for the cardinals and woodpeckers,

the ordinary sparrows;
the goldfinches won't come here anymore—
I don't think I ever saw one.

Hunting Creek

where the trees are the deepest green
Hunting Creek runs
parallel to the road that bears its name
there on its banks where the corn grows
tall overnight
like a teenage boy you haven't seen in years
there—right there—lies part of my soul

I'm not sure why it has settled on that place in particular
but who can reason where souls are concerned?

I know only that it's chosen that spot
in the shadow of the hickories
in the field where families of deer gather to eat yellow corn
while crying crows wheel overhead

not home, exactly
for my soul has no place it feels at home
but perhaps as a place to haunt when I am gone
and the trees remain

The Ship and the Storm

my other life began   when you awoke
with a mast on the horizon   and the ship had left
the one I wanted   to take you home
though it didn't matter   you chose silence
that quiet moment   the storm
answered my question   said all you needed
and on that shore   I glimpsed a version of you
contained within my memories that existed long before
I was born from the waves   you turned against the tide
what a strange garden   what the heart cultivates
is the sea   a thing to be harvested
full of flowers we cannot pick blooming with belief and blame
and colors invisible   that we never truly see
in the dark of the deep   until they are gone

PUBLICATION CREDITS

For Dave, "Magnolia Blooms" was previously published in *hand picked poetry*. "Last Night, I Dreamed of the Korengal," "Look at This Thing We've Made," and "War Poetry" were previously published, in different forms, in *Wrath-Bearing Tree*.

For Diane, "Artless Man" was previously published in *Vita Brevis*; "On a Whim" in *Kissing Dynamite*; "Flower Bud" in *The Hellebore*; "Things I Never Want to Understand" in *The Interpreter's House*; "The Way You Talk About War" in *Crêpe & Penn*; "Bodies" and "Brood Parasite" in *Visitant*; "Makeup Palette" and "A Study in Lavender" in *Cypress*; "Find Me a Savior" in *Ample Remains*; "Micro Expressions" in *Invisible City*; "Care Instructions" in *The Emerson Review*; and "the patterns, the contradictions" and "You find an apology letter on your windshield" in the *Common Threads* anthologies from the Ohio Poetry Association.

ACKNOWLEDGMENTS

We're immensely grateful to the Greater Columbus Arts Council and all supporters of the arts in Columbus for awarding us the Artist Projects Grant that made this collection possible. With these funds, we had the joy of working with Emily Morgan on the original collage cover art and two wonderful editors, David G. Clark and Ella Maoz. We were grateful to have Levi Gaidos as our trusty cover designer, Melissa Dias-Mandoly as our expert typesetter, and Jordan Riley Swan of Story Garden Publishing as our distributor and vessel for all our publishing woes.

Diane:

Dave once told me, half-jokingly, "What's great about you is you're not afraid to be wrong." I've never been more thankful to be wrong when it came to our odds of receiving the grant for this project (and perhaps a few other things). Thank you for always believing in us and in me as my partner in life and in story.

Much love to my family members who have supported my writing since I was a child. My mom framed the first poem I ever wrote at eight years old about an existential snowflake that said, "I wonder where I am in this world." Not much has changed.

To Steven—thank you for being in my life. Sending hugs to all the friends, past and present, whom I have written poems for and about in this collection, with Jeanie getting the most hugs of all.

Many thanks to the Ohio Poetry Association and all the literary magazines that have provided homes to my poems across the years, gifting me the external validation I needed to finally call myself a poet. And my heart is full for everyone I work with at Urban Arts Space, a one-of-a-kind community that has enriched my creative life.

Dave:

First, I want to thank Diane, whose love, words, and poems I never want to be without, and whose vision made this collection possible. Next, I want to acknowledge Edmund and Evelyn, whose laughter and kindness make me so proud to be your dad. I also want to express my gratitude to all the people in my life who have given me the kind of support that saves lives, most of all to Christy, but also Bobby G. and Bobby G., Nate Allen, Curtis Rohrscheib, Patrick Montes, Brian Barkman, Terrance Oliver, and Falefa Tagoilelagi. Finally, to Robert Hoyt—we still love you, just like we did that day.

ABOUT THE AUTHORS

Diane Callahan is a writer and editor who also happens to work at an art gallery. On her YouTube channel, *Quotidian Writer*, she provides advice for aspiring authors. She serves as the managing editor for Story Garden Publishing and was the former fiction editor for *Consequence*, a literary magazine centered on the consequences of war.

David Dixon is a father, veteran, and writer whose poetry appears in *hand picked poetry* and *Wrath-Bearing Tree*. His short fiction has been featured in several anthologies, and his science fiction series, Black Sun, was published by Dark Brew Press.

www.ingramcontent.com/pod-product-compliance
Lightning Source LLC
Chambersburg PA
CBHW030920140626
46545CB00016B/2336